It's Catching

Warts

Angela Royston

Designed by David Oakley/Arnos Design
Originated by Dot Gradations
Printed in Hong Kong, China

06 05 04 03 02
10 9 8 7 6 5 4 3 2

Library of Congress Cataloging-in-Publication Data
Royston, Angela.
    Warts / Angela Royston.
        p. ; cm. -- (It's catching)
    Includes bibliographical references and index.
    ISBN 1-58810-231-9
    1. Warts--Juvenile literature. [1. Warts.]
    [DNLM: 1. Warts--transmission--Juvenile Literature. 2.
    Warts--prevention & control--Juvenile Literature. WC 570 R892w 2001]
    I. Title. II. Series.

RL471 .R695 2001
616.5'44--dc21
                            00-012836

Acknowledgments
The Publishers would like to thank the following for permission to reproduce photographs:
p. 13 Ian West/Bubbles; p. 12 The Purcell Team/Corbis; pp. 6, 17, 18, 20, 23 Gareth Boden; p. 27 Images colour library; pp. 4, 5, 19, 22, 24, 25 Martin Soukias; p. 26 Zefa/Powerstock; p. 10 Robert Harding; p. 21 Sally and Richard Greenhill; Science Photo Library: pp. 7 Quest, 8 Sinclair Stammers, 9 Clinique Ste Catherine, 11 Mark Clarke, 14, 15, 16 P. Marazzi; p. 29 Amwell/Stone; p. 28 Telegraph colour library.

Cover photograph reproduced with permission of Science Photo Library.

BAND-AID ® is a registered trademark of JOHNSON & JOHNSON.

Every effort has been made to contact copyright holders of any material reproduced in this book. Any omissions will be rectified in subsequent printings if notice is given to the Publisher.

Some words are shown in bold, **like this.** You can find out what they mean by looking in the glossary.

Contents

What Are Warts?

Warts are small bumps in the skin on your face or hands caused by a **virus.** Plantar warts are warts that affect the skin on the bottom of your feet.

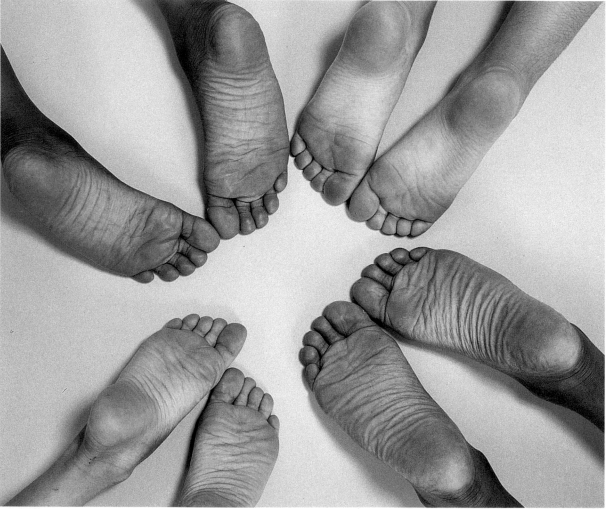

Warts and plantar warts are not serious, but they can be uncomfortable. This book looks at what causes warts, how they are spread, and how they can be treated.

Healthy Skin

Skin covers your whole body like a stretchy wrapper. It keeps dirt, **germs,** and other harmful things from getting inside your body.

The outer layer of skin is made of tiny, hard flakes. This is what skin looks like under a **microscope.**

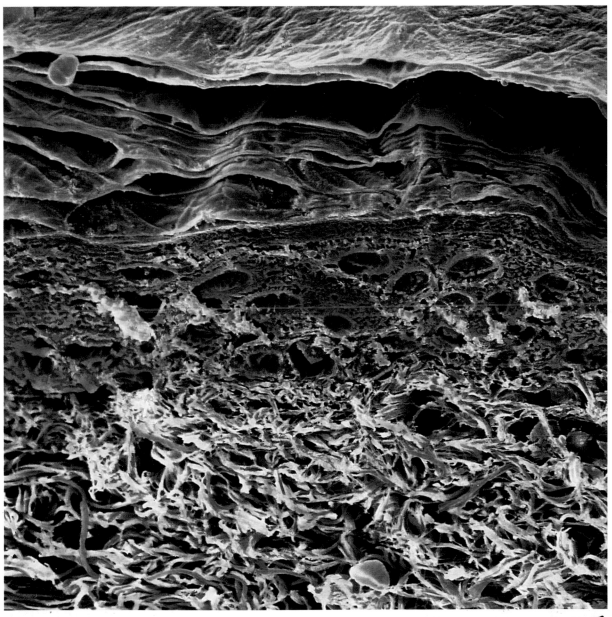

What Causes Illness?

Many illnesses are caused by **germs** called **bacteria** or by **viruses.** Germs are so small that they can only be seen through a powerful **microscope.**

This is the virus that causes warts and plantar warts. Each wart contains millions of wart viruses. They can be passed from one person to another.

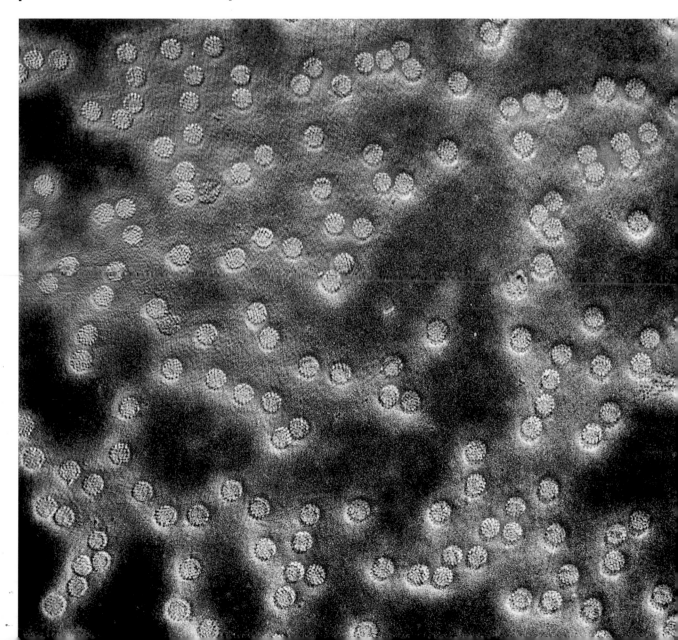

How Do You Catch Warts?

When an illness can be passed from one person to another, we say it is catching or **infectious.** To catch warts, you have to touch the **virus.**

The virus gets into the body through cuts
or breaks in the outer layer of the skin.
It is important to keep cuts clean and
covered up as much as you can.

Catching Plantar Warts

Warts on the hands and face are not very **infectious.** You can catch plantar warts more easily. You catch them by walking on the **virus** in bare feet.

Do not touch your own wart or plantar wart. If you touch it, you can spread it to another part of your skin.

What Do Warts Look Like?

Warts may be rough or smooth. Sometimes the skin around them turns a bit darker than the rest of the skin. Most warts do not hurt.

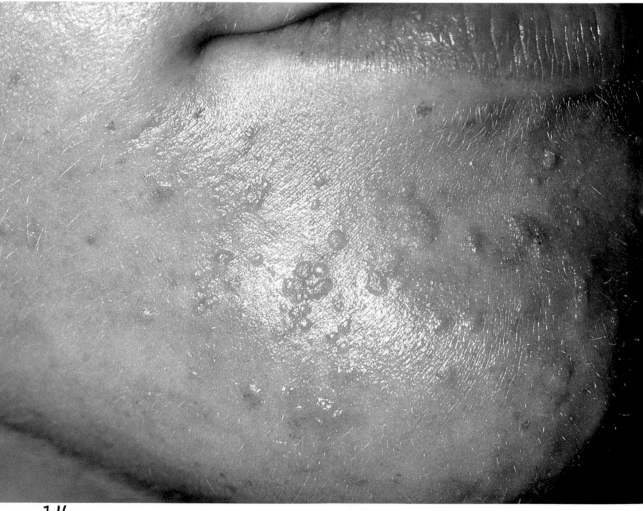

Warts may take months before they appear. They will eventually go away on their own as your body kills the **virus.**

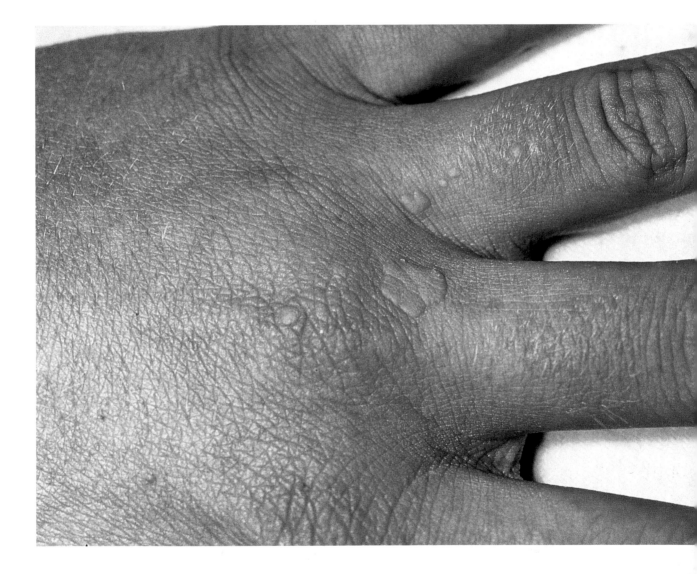

What Do Plantar Warts Look Like?

Plantar warts appear on your feet and feel rougher than the other skin. They also usually have a black spot in the middle.

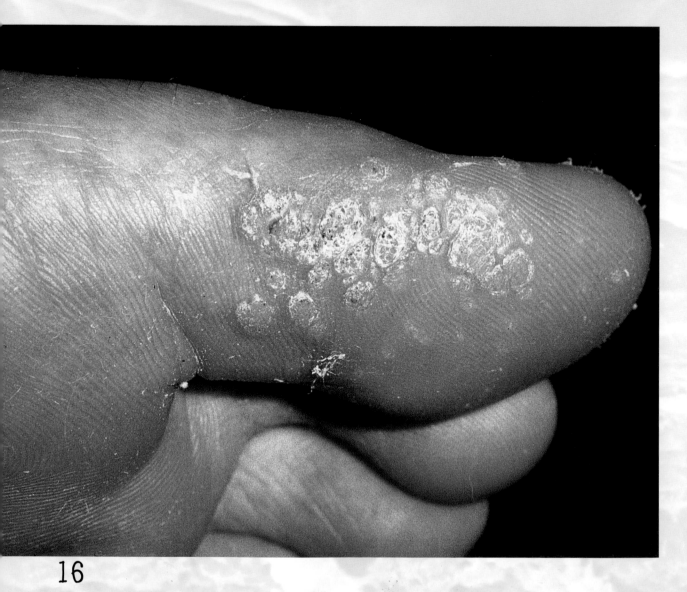

If you do not treat a plantar wart, you may soon have several more. Some large plantar warts go deep into the skin. They become very painful to walk on.

Treatment

Pharmacists sell many different **ointments** for treating warts and plantar warts. The ointment is rubbed onto the wart. Follow the instructions carefully.

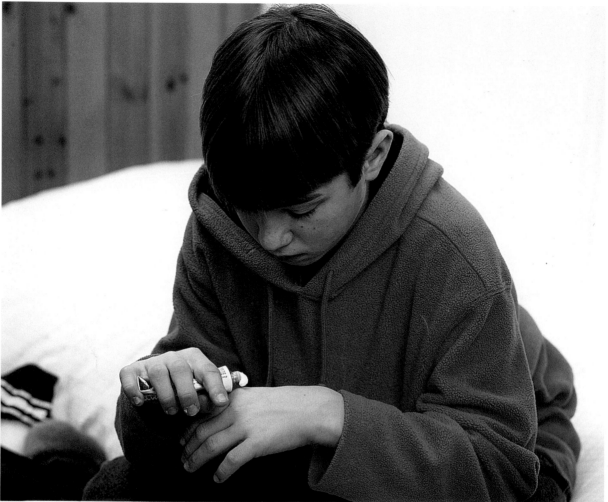

The ointment slowly kills the skin around the wart, but it may take several weeks to work. The wart may also have to be covered with a Band-Aid.®

Other Treatments

Some **herbal remedies** are gentler than **ointments.** Ask an adult if you want to try to find one that works.

Some warts and plantar warts are hard to get rid of. Then a doctor may decide to **freeze** the wart off or use a **laser** to remove it.

How To Avoid Warts

If you want to avoid warts and plantar warts, wash your feet and hands often. Don't suck on pens or your thumb and don't use anyone else's towel. Shower before and after you swim.

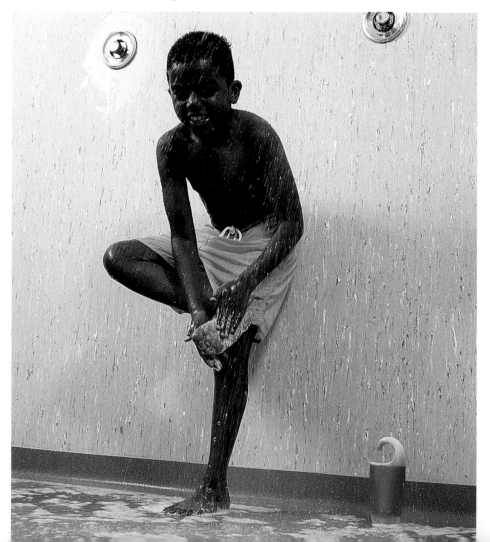

Remember, wart **viruses** can only affect you if the skin is broken. Cover up cuts and **grazes** to keep the virus out.

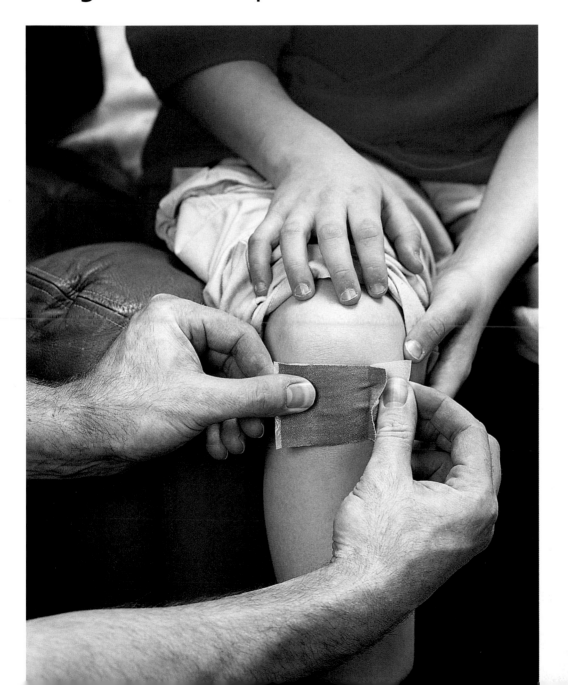

Don't Spread Warts!

If you have warts or plantar warts, don't let other people borrow your towel. Don't let them wear your gloves or flip-flops.

Don't run around in bare feet if you have a plantar wart. You can still go swimming, but you should wear a waterproof sock.

Staying Healthy

If you are healthy, you are less likely to get sick. Eating plenty of fruit and raw vegetables helps your body fight and kill **viruses.**

Getting plenty of exercise and keeping
clean also help you to stay healthy.
Wash your hands often and wear
clean clothes.

Think About It!

Suppose one of these children has warts on his or her hands. How might the wart **viruses** spread from one child to another?*

If one of these children has plantar warts, how can that child help keep the other children from catching them?*

*Read page 30 to find out.

Answers

Page 28

Some of the wart **viruses** might rub off onto the ball. When the other children catch the ball, some of the viruses will stick to their hands. If there is a break in the skin on any of their hands, the virus may infect them.

Page 29

If one of the children has plantar warts, he or she should wear a waterproof sock on the infected foot. You should always shower before and after swimming whether you have plantar warts or not.

Stay Healthy and Safe!

1. Always tell an adult if you feel sick or think there is something wrong with you.

2. Never take any **medicine** or use any **ointment** unless it is given to you by an adult you trust.

3. Remember, the best way to stay healthy and safe is to eat good food, drink lots of water, keep clean, exercise, and get lots of sleep.

Glossary

bacteria   tiny living thing that is usually harmless, but can make you sick if it gets inside your body

freeze   make very cold; when living things, such as viruses, become very cold they die

germ   tiny living thing that makes you sick if it gets inside your body

graze   scrape or scratch of the skin

herbal remedy   medicine made from plants

infectious   can be passed from one person to another and can make you sick

laser   very narrow beam of strong light; doctors use lasers to burn or cut parts of the body

medicine   something used to treat or prevent an illness

microscope   something that makes very small things look big enough to see

ointment   oily cream that often contains medicine and is rubbed onto the skin

pharmacists   people who sell medicines and things that you usually use in the bathroom

virus   living thing even smaller than bacteria that can make you sick if it gets inside your body

Index

More Books to Read

Hundley, David H. *Viruses*. Vero Beach, Fla.: Rourke Press, 1998.

Kinch, Michael P. *Warts*. Danbury, Conn.: Franklin Watts, 2000.

Royston, Angela. *Clean and Healthy*. Chicago: Heinemann Library, 1999.